Blood of the Air

THE DRINKING GOURD CHAPBOOK POETRY PRIZE

Blood of the Air

Poems

Ama Codjoe

NORTHWESTERN UNIVERSITY PRESS

EVANSTON, ILLINOIS

Northwestern University Press
www.nupress.northwestern.edu

Northwestern University Poetry and Poetics Colloquium
www.poetry.northwestern.edu

Printed in the United States of America

10   9   8   7   6   5   4   3   2   1

Library of Congress Cataloging-in-Publication Data
Names: Codjoe, Ama, 1979– author.
Title: Blood of the air : poems / Ama Codjoe.
Other titles: Drinking gourd chapbook poetry prize.
Description: Evanston, Illinois : Northwestern University Press, 2020. |
Series: Drinking Gourd Chapbook poetry prize.
Identifiers: LCCN 2019042371 | ISBN 9780810141711 (trade paperback)
Subjects: LCGFT: Poetry.
Classification: LCC PS3603.O2954 A6 2020 | DDC 811.6—dc23
LC record available at https://lccn.loc.gov/2019042371

now I can see
I have been carrying this
fear
a blue thing
the length of my life asking *Is this*
its place
bringing it here

—W. S. MERWIN, "THE BIRDS ON THE MORNING OF GOING"

Contents

Foreword

Ed Roberson

The eponymous poem of Ama Codjoe's collection refers to the actions of the Greek god Zeus in relationship to Leda. The poet Codjoe brings to our attention how ambiguously the god's intentions—and so his responsibility—are rendered, and therefore, regarded. Throughout this remarkable collection, she makes it clear that it is not just gods, but we mortals who abuse power—even the power of storytelling.

In her poem, "She Said," Codjoe graphically enacts the textured silences that surround violation and the willful failure to listen. She poetically figures the inner lives of women swept up by the violence of political events, like Betty Shabazz, or swept up by the power of individual lust, like Leda, or swept up by the public's will of its story, like the woman who dances herself to death in Pina Bausch's *The Rite of Spring*.

But Codjoe does not always let her women be swept up, under, or aside. In these blood-tinged poems, she takes up the final question in W. B. Yeats's "Leda and the Swan," "Did she put on his knowledge with his power / Before the indifferent beak could let her drop?" The figures of Betty Davis, Betye Saar's Aunt Jemima, and—as evidenced by the book you are holding—the poet herself, are raging fierce assertions, whether heard or not, whether listened to or not.

Her voice says she "gonna try on [her] nakedness like a silk kimono," "climb the men who, when they see [her] face, turn into stony mountains," and that she "*ain't gonna study war no more*" . . .

Yes, listen. Listen. Ama Codjoe's writing is too eloquent not to hear.

Acknowledgments

This book is dedicated to my teachers and to my mother—my first teacher.

I bow deeply to every friend, tree, mentor, and sister who has supported me. I would like to thank the following institutions—and the people guiding them—for the continued faith they've shown in my work: Cave Canem Foundation, the Callaloo Creative Writing Workshop, New York University's Graduate Creative Writing Program, and the Rona Jaffe Foundation. I would also like to record my thanks to Crosstown Arts for providing the residency where I wrote this book.

Boundless gratitude to the Poetry and Poetics Colloquium at Northwestern University and to the judges of the 2019 Drinking Gourd Chapbook Poetry Prize: Chris Abani, John Alba Cutler, Reginald Gibbons, Susannah Young-ah Gottlieb, Ed Roberson, and Natasha Trethewey. And again to Ed Roberson for generously writing the foreword. I would also like to thank Parneshia Jones, Anne Gendler, and the entire team at Northwestern University Press for helping usher *Blood of the Air* from my hands into yours.

Finally, grateful acknowledgment to John Hennessy of *The Common* for originally publishing "Burying Seeds," winner of the 2019 DISQUIET Literary Prize, and "The Beekeeper's Husband."

Blood of the Air

Burying Seeds

for Betty Shabazz

Who, when they killed her husband, was carrying
twin girls—not in her arms, but in an armless
sea, with bits of blood as food. She covered

her daughters in the waters of her body.
She covered her daughters in the rooms
her body built, pressed against the wooden

floor of the Audubon Ballroom. She must have
cried, as my mother did, when she stuttered, *Twins?*
into the paper gown of the hospital room.

The body longs for its double. Even twins
stretch long their arms toward other strangers.
The first time I visited a mosque, I was surprised

to be separated from my father and brothers.
I sat, with the women and girls, alone.
From across the aisle, I stared at the men

longingly. As a child, I asked my preschool teacher
why I couldn't play outside, shirtless like
the boys. It was a hot day. Before she could answer,

I relented, wearing my favorite undershirt—the one
with Archie, Betty, and Veronica—chasing
my sun-kissed brothers across the playground.

Lately, when I glimpse my nakedness in the half
mirror above the bathroom sink, I'm looking
at the photograph of Pauline Lumumba baring

her breasts as a sign of mourning. The widow's
breasts and mine hang like four weeping eyes,
without titillation, fertility, or innocence.

I wanted to write a poem for Betty Shabazz
because her high cheekbones and luminous
eyes are like a BaKongo mask breathed

into with life. After her husband's lifeless
body was wrapped in white linen and covered
by the words: *what we place in the ground*

is no more now a man—but a seed—she took one
last look at him who *had* smiled at her
and touched, countless times, her unveiled face.

My mother did not wear a veil on her wedding day.
Eighteen years after their divorce, my father
fidgets with the gold band she slid along his finger.

As she made a circle with her thumb and forefinger,
shimmying the ring over my father's knuckle,
which words did her mind circle over: *worse* or *better*

death or *death*? That night, did my mother bunch
the hotel bedsheet in one hand like a nosegay?
Did she allow it—another white dress—to drag,

crumpled, behind her? The vows we promise
one another are veils through which we envision
the future; we enact our dreams using a vision

clouded by tulle and lace. Grief-stricken, Betty Shabazz
said of her husband's assassination, *Well, it finally
happened*. Weeks prior, she had taken to wearing

her husband's hat for comfort and continued to do so
after he died. I want a desire that could be mistaken
for grief to cloud my face, to make me shudder, to twist

my mouth into a cry. Once, I shared a bed with a man
who, as a boy, heard his parents' lovemaking. *I was
confused*, he admitted, *it sounded like they were in pain.*

Grief is the bride of every good thing, Betty Shabazz
reminds me. I'm wearing a veil the shape of a waterfall,
which is also the shape of my mother's dress falling

from her shoulders. Through its fabric, I can see a cloud
turning into a horse and a plane that could be a star—
a star that might be a planet. It's hard to tell from here,

wrapped in the caul of the present, fixed on this plot
of grass, with so many seeds buried underground,
and winter—forged into a circle—threatening never to end.

Head on Ice #5

after Lorna Simpson

She's cold as a snake
She'll cut you
She was dreaming
Her face had been cut out of a magazine
Of ice formations
The color of sapphire
She wasn't cut out to be a housewife
She undressed in the middle of the night
She wasn't cut out to be a soccer mom
She was hot
And kicked off the covers
She saw him disappear by the river
She peeled the apple skin
Into one long ribbon
Until she lay naked
In the grass
She wasn't cut out to be a den mother
Her hands were cold
Only to discount her memory
She's cold-hearted
She had always wanted ice sculptures
At her wedding
They asked her to tell
What happened
Of swans
Her hands were cold as ice
They asked her to tell what happened
Only to discount
Her memory

At least
He didn't
Cut her face
She wore a sapphire ring
Because
You know
All that trouble with diamonds
The jeweler spoke of a classic cut
She was cold-blooded
Memory fell like a bang
Over her eye
She was streaked with melting
On her head
She wore a glacier
Drifting
Like a wig

Blood of the Air

Touch is probably the single sensual realm that most defines the difference between enslaved and free—or I suppose we could say enslaved and relatively free.

—HORTENSE SPILLERS, "SHADES OF INTIMACY"

1. When Zeus saw her, he fell in love with her. He transformed into a swan and appeared in

2. front of her; he seduced her and slept with her.

3. Leda was admired by Zeus, who seduced her in the guise of a swan. As a swan, Zeus fell into

4. her arms for protection from a pursuing eagle.

5. Leda was a beautiful woman, and her beauty attracted the attention of Zeus, who spied her

6. from his throne on Mount Olympus. The beauty of Leda roused Zeus to action, and the God

7. transformed himself into a magnificent swan. Then, portraying himself as a bird escaping

8. from a bird of prey, Zeus lay down next to Leda, and impregnated her.

9. She was seduced by Zeus in the shape of a swan.

10. According to the common legend Zeus visited Leda in the disguise of a swan, and she

11. produced two eggs . . .

12. Zeus in the form of a swan consorted with Leda . . .

13. Zeus, father of the gods, fell in love with the beautiful Leda and, when rejected by her,

14. turned himself into a swan.

She Said

Hello

Can you hear me

Can you hear me now

Hello

I can't hear you

I'm sorry you're breaking up

Is this better

Can you hear me now

Hello

Hello

Can you hear me now

Hello

*

And the said Agostino retorted that . . . [hole in page] and that he should find it, that otherwise he would have . . . [hole in page] for this ugly . . . [holes in page]

[[20. How long after it happened [did you tell]? Why didn't you tell it immediately, and, if immediately, why didn't you bring suit? Why have you said it now and what induced you to say it?]]

To the twentieth, she said

To the twenty-first, she said

To the twenty-second, she said

To the tenth one she answered as above

To the twelfth, she referred to the next one

And to the first [question] she answered

And while they were writing this down

To the third one she answered

To the thirteenth, she answered

To the eighth one she said

And the said summoned woman answered

*

FOOTNOTE 58: Hole in the page, one or two words missing.

FOOTNOTE 51: Hole in the page; three words missing.

I'm sorry you're breaking—

She was asked

She answered

FOOTNOTE 68: The page is torn; two or three words are missing at the beginning of the line, and a line or more is cut off at the bottom of the page.

The said summoned woman retorting

Can you—

FOOTNOTE 63: See ms. 10.

*

And while the guard tightened the said cords with a running string, the said woman began to say

Then the judge, having heard [all this], etc., terminated the interrogation and ordered that the witness be sent back to her house for the time being.

*

When considering this poem, I know the "I" is missing. Twelve years ago, on one occasion, [ ] was robbed, assaulted, and almost raped by the same man, a stranger.

*

Is this better

FOOTNOTE 26: Literally, "lying in his throat" (mentirà per la gola).

How about now

The connection is bad

Sorry

Hold on

Hold on

Literally, "lying in his throat"

How about now

How

repeating the above words over and over, and then saying,

o

sorry

breaking

Hell

o

sorry

about

no

now

o

Hell

He

better

hear

breaking

break

better

be

breaking

this

can't

me

the *hear* in hearing the *ear* the *he* the *he* in she the *sh* in shame the *me* the shh in me the ssshhhhh the *y* in saying the why the *say* the said the sad the sad *i* the scared *i* terrified she tried to say the *test* in testify the *be* in believed the *lie* the lived the silent *i* the why in silence the shh in she the *she* before the space before the space between *she* and *said* the *ears* in years the saying the said between

*

She added afterward voluntarily

She answered

She added afterward voluntarily

She added afterward

She added afterward voluntarily

She answered

She answered

She added afterward voluntarily

*

"At this point, I will do my best to answer your questions."

*

FOOTNOTE 70: Page is torn; a final line not legible.

Poem After Betye Saar's *The Liberation of Aunt Jemima*

What if, Betye, instead of a rifle or hand
grenade—I mean, what if after
the loaded gun that takes two hands
to fire, I lay down the splintered broom
and the steel so cold it wets
my cheek? What if I unclench the valleys
of my fist, and lay down
the wailing baby?
Gonna burn the moon in a cast-iron skillet.
Gonna climb the men who, when they see my face, turn into stony
    mountains.
Gonna get out of the kitchen.
Gonna try on my nakedness like a silk kimono.
Gonna find me a lover who eats nothing but pussy.
Let the whites of my eyes roll, roll.
Gonna clench my toes.
Gonna purr beneath my own hand.
Gonna take down my hair.
Try on a crown of crow feathers.
Gonna roam the wide aisles of the peach grove, light dripping off
    branches like syrup, leaves brushing the fuzz on my arms.
—You dig?—
Gonna let the juice trickle down my chin.
Gonna smear the sun like war paint across my chest.
Gonna shimmy into a pair of royal blue bell-bottoms.
Gonna trample the far-out thunderclouds, heavy in their lightness.
Watch them slink away.
Gonna grimace. Gonna grin.
Gonna lay down my sword.
Pick up the delicate eggs of my fists.
Gonna jab the face that hovered over mine.
It's easy to find the lips, surrounded as they are in minstrel black.

Gonna bloody the head of every god, ghost, or swan who has torn into
    me—pried me open with its beak.
Gonna catch my breath in a hunting trap.
Gonna lean against the ropes.
Gonna break the nose of mythology.
—Goodnight John-Boy—
Gonna ice my hands in April's stream.
Gonna scowl and scream and shepherd my hollering into a green pasture.
Gonna mend my annihilations into a white picket fence.
Gonna whip a tornado with my scarlet handkerchief.
Spin myself dizzy as a purple-lipped drunkard.
Gonna lay down, by the riverside, sticky and braless in the golden sand.
Ain't gonna study war no more.
Ain't gonna study war no more.
Ain't gonna study war no more.

Found Poem #4

Dear Betty Crocker:
On your advice, I went ahead
and made the angel food cake mix
that we found in our bomb shelter.
It rose just beautifully.
You were right. It worked
after all these years
because it was stored in a cool,
dry place.

The Beekeeper's Husband

You used pine straw as fuel to smoke the bees
    deeper into the hive, compelling them to engorge

their abdomens with honey. I could smell the sweat
    gathering under your bra. I wanted to lick

the salty rivulets. How could I not be moved
    by the sight of your wrists, exposed?

After I chewed the golden wax
    like a plant surviving on light, after you lost

two colonies to varroa, one after the other,
    after you caught, all told, a dozen swarms

of the neighbor's bees, I realized,
    after it all, that when you spoke so low

it was hard to distinguish praying from cursing
    from singing, you weren't talking to yourself

or to the bees—as I long believed—
    but to a god you no longer feared.

When, on the day we met, I stooped
    to kiss your ungloved hand, you mistook

me for a gallant: someone who hungers
    for sweetness. My dear wife, from the first,

it was salt I craved. This is the gesture that began
    our troubles; though you believe it was the night—

years later, years ago—when I asked why, if you
        trusted me, you never undressed completely.

With the bees you donned a veil, and with me,
        I insisted, you wore a second skin the texture

of bark. It scorched my hands to touch.
        When I told you this, we were lying in bed,

recovering from giving whatever we could.
        You turned your naked back to me.

Outside a siren wailed and faded.
        That night, I slept soundly, sprawled

on top of the sheets. I dreamt I was wingless
        and beautiful, treading water in a crystal blue sea.

When I woke the next morning, ashen twigs
        and brittle leaves lay scattered on your pillow.

Found Poem #3

Dear Betty Crocker:
We are on safari in Africa.
How the women who live
on remote farms in Kenya find
the time and energy to devote
to the finer points of baking
while dealing with invading lions,
leopards and locust plagues
is remarkable. But they complain
that the lightness and texture
of the cakes they bake need
improvement. The flour used
here is simply ground wheat,
not as fine nor white
as General Mills Softasilk
cake flour. Could you possible
[*sic*] tell us, if it is not a trade
secret, what might be done
to improve the quality
of the Kenya flour?
Your assistance would be
extremely welcome, both
for its intrinsic value
and as a gesture of
American kindness.

Detail from "Poem After Betye Saar's *The Liberation of Aunt Jemima*"

And out of her gushing head, I witnessed
four fully-grown women spring forth
like winged beasts: the first woman
wore the charm of her unmasked hair
and a taken-for-granted beauty that made
her all the more enticing; the last woman
modeled an anonymous version of herself—
an "I" that didn't remind anyone
of anyone else, but who reminded Aunt Jemima
of freedom; the second woman brandished
a handheld mirror she spat on
then polished with the ruffled hem
of her apron, a mirror all the women,
except the last, gathered around
like campfire; and the second to last
woman carried a pink mulatto, squirming
on her hip—in the baby's hand a rattle,
in the rattle a shattered lightbulb,
in the filament, a portrait
of the child's father, who some say
Aunt Jemima tempted with her bottle-shaped
hips, but who was known to be monstrous—
a so-called god—and I beheld a sea
of blood, dark as syrup, oozing
from Aunt Jemima's neck,
and four women flying, without shoes
or wings, from her maternal, amber body.

Nasty Woman

Inside me a nasty gal growls like the gravel racing
beneath a motorcycle, louder than the engine

chirring inside. "There's always been a bird inside
me," Betty Davis said. And because I've learned

to decipher one black bird in a mob of black birds,
I know the bird inside her inside me is neither

raven nor blackbird nor grackle. I can tell
by the way it caws inside the nasty gal's

lusty snarl: the bird inside her inside me
is crow. Carrion rots further in crow's gizzard.

Sometimes the dead animal is love.
Sometimes I offer a part of myself:

carcass on the believer's tongue.
Yesterday, I fed crow three names written

in blue ink on torn notebook paper.
The day before, an idea of myself died.

Crow devoured it greedily. The Betty inside me
rasps and howls, wearing a zebra-print leotard,

straddling the rungs of my ribs, and blowing
into the ram-like horns of my uterus.

Betty dines on what's alive. Electric guitar,
gray suede shoes. Lewd as an unchaste nude.

Vulgar as a seasick sailor steering a tempest-tossed
ship. Nasty as funk. Funky as an armpit.

Gritty as grits. Filthy as the back of your mama's
neck. Raw as sushi. Raw as Eddie Murphy.

Pitifully nasty. Nasty as graffiti in the men's
locker room. Betty loves to hear the story

of Artemis, the virgin goddess, who as punishment
for ogling at her river-cleaned pubis,

transformed Actaeon into a stag and watched
his own pack of hounds tear him

to smithereens. Betty can live off that story
for weeks. That and chocolate ice cream.

The Betty inside me licks her lips suggestively.
She's got a foul mouth, and glorious teeth,

and a beak as sharp as a sword. Inside me
is a nasty gal housed by a nastier woman.

Le sacre du printemps

after Pina Bausch

At this time of night, the theater is empty:
draped in its velvet robes, echoing with ghosts

and applause. I've been tossing and turning
all night, as headlights flash across the ceiling.

Inside the ornate opera house, it felt close to midnight—
bottomless like tonight—though it was the middle

of the day when I arrived and the usher
escorted me to my seat. An ocean of dirt

covered the stage. The dancers performed
underneath and on top of Stravinsky's score.

With their bodies, they made another music:
full of lunges, panting, slaps, stomps,

and whatever sounds the body makes
when it yields to unyielding earth.

Men and women threw themselves on the floor
and into each other: smearing their skins

with dirt, violence, and sweat.
I am restless. Tonight, I remember

I vowed to feel as alive as the woman who—
in a rite of spring—must dance herself

to death. Hair frazzled, clothes soiled, the fated
woman fell to the earth then sprang back up,

slashing the air and contracting her body as if
she'd been punched repeatedly. She fell

and danced, danced and fell, until she collapsed
for the last time. —The stage went black.—

How quickly I walked into the bright day,
leaving her there, behind me. On nights

like this one, when I'm crazed by wakefulness,
and darkness sacrifices itself, anxious limb

by anxious limb, into the day's endless mouth,
I take the red dress from the dead woman's body

and dance wildly, with such abandon,
all that's left is dream.

Notes

"Burying Seeds": Some italicized words in this poem come from Ossie Davis's eulogy of Malcolm X, delivered on February 27, 1965, at the Faith Temple Church of God and Christ in Harlem; other italicized words are from an interview of Betty Shabazz by Mal Goode of ABC News, conducted shortly after her husband's assassination.

"Head on Ice #5": The poem is titled after a 2016 painting by Lorna Simpson. Italicized phrases are taken from text accompanying Simpson's 1986 photograph "Waterbearer."

"Blood of the Air": Language in this poem is mined from an internet search of "Leda" and imported verbatim from various online sources.
   The epigraph comes from Dr. Hortense Spillers's keynote, "Shades of Intimacy: Women in the Time of Revolution," delivered at Cornell University on March 18, 2016.
   The title borrows a phrase from W. B. Yeats's sonnet "Leda and the Swan."

"She Said": Italicized and quoted language in this poem are taken from the transcript in "Testimony of the Rape Trial of 1612" from *Artemisia Gentileschi* by Mary D. Garrard and from Dr. Christine Blasey Ford's written testimony delivered to the United States Senate Judiciary Committee on September 26, 2018, which concludes: "At this point, I will do my best to answer your questions."

"Poem After Betye Saar's *The Liberation of Aunt Jemima*": The engine of the poem and the concluding italicized phrases are taken from the spiritual "Down by the Riverside."

"Found Poem #4": A call addressed to Betty Crocker with the attribution "Call back from Arizona, 1990" from "Letters to Betty Crocker." *Betty Crocker*, www.bettycrocker.com/menus-holidays-parties/mhplibrary /parties-and-get-togethers/vintage-betty/letters-to-betty-crocker.

"Found Poem #3": A letter addressed to Betty Crocker with the attribution "Letter from Mrs. Ernest Hemingway Kimama Swamp, Kenya, 1954." Ibid.

"Nasty Woman": The Betty Davis quote is taken from the film *Betty: They Say I'm Different* (2017).

Ama Codjoe has been awarded support from the Cave Canem, Salton-stall, Jerome, and Robert Rauschenberg Foundations as well as from the Callaloo Creative Writing Workshop, Crosstown Arts, Hedgebrook, and the MacDowell Colony. Her poems have appeared in *The Common*, *Massachusetts Review*, *Southern Indiana Review*, and elsewhere. Codjoe is the recipient of a 2017 Rona Jaffe Writer's Award, the *Georgia Review*'s 2018 Loraine Williams Poetry Prize, a 2019 DISQUIET Literary Prize, and a 2019 NEA Creative Writing Fellowship.